TUNED IN

EIGHT LESSONS TO SALES SUCCESS
A Great Salesman Did Not Know He Knew

Stacey Alcorn

AuthorHouse™
1663 Liberty Drive
Bloomington, IN 47403
www.authorhouse.com
Phone: 1-800-839-8640

First published by AuthorHouse 6/22/2011

ISBN: 978-1-4567-3151-9 (sc)
ISBN: 978-1-4567-3152-6 (e)

Library of Congress Control Number: 2011900620

Printed in the United States of America

ACKNOWLEDGMENTS

This book is dedicated to all the people that inspire me.

To my family who has taught me that to make the best use of resources, we must provide opportunity for others. Capital gives us the power to even the playing field for all.

To Ed who has inspired me to put up a good fight in any and all of life's challenges. Mohamed Ali has nothing on you.

To Jay and Oshyn who have taught a self proclaimed workaholic that the only thing better than the fun and exhilaration of the day to day toil is coming home at night to be with the family.

And to the hundreds of agents and staff members that inspire me daily. You have taught me the fine art of getting back up.

CONTENTS

FOREWORD

by Dave Liniger –
Founder and Chairman
RE/MAX, LLC

General George Patton once said, "Accept the challenges so that you may feel the exhilaration of victory." There is no doubt about it, we have faced some challenging times as humans these past few years. Terrorism is a worldwide threat to peaceful civilization. Countries remain at war over protecting borders, religions, and political affiliations. The United States economy continues to stall while foreclosure and jobless rates inch up and median home prices and unit sales inch down. Being a business leader, sales person, or entrepreneur, in this market is not for the faint of heart.

For the fearless, determined, and confident, there lay something wonderful hidden amongst the ashes of exigent times. Here lay opportunity. There are business leaders, sales people, and entrepreneurs that see beyond the news reports and market data, beyond the negativity and trepidation to a world ripe with opportunity. Millionaires are being made by the minute, if not by the second. Look around you. For they are the ones who continue to find the silver lining in the midst of the upheaval. They find opportunity where others see just bedlam.

Tuned In – Eight Lessons To Sales Success A Great Salesman Did Not Know He Knew is a parable that every business person should read and embrace. It is with this mindset of resilience, determination, and finding opportunity where others have stopped looking that enabled me to build the largest real estate organization in the world. This book is about how to adopt that same mindset in your own business and life. This is the story of finding the silver lining...opportunity...and your way to greatness and triumph no matter what happens in the world around you. Embrace these simple lessons and you will have beat any market making you and your business recession-proof. So, shut off the television, close your ears to the news, and get *Tuned In* for a great story.

Dave Liniger

Founder and Chairman RE/MAX, LLC

Tuned In

Eight Lessons To Sales Success A Great Salesman Did Not Know He Knew

Stacey Alcorn

CHAPTER 1 –

SUMMER

It was a Saturday morning and Barney Hasbin was heading to work at nine o'clock, but not because he wanted to. His manager, Summer Straus, had called him the evening before and said it was urgent that they meet first thing Saturday. Barney had worked for First Call Realty for nineteen years now and never had his sales production been so low. The real estate market in Dundee Falls was crushed, with sales volume down 29% from four years earlier. With unemployment still rising, crime rates up, and sellers giving their homes back to the banks that held the mortgages, there seemed to be no light at the end of the tunnel.

It was October first and Barney had only sold three homes all year. In the heyday he would sell three houses a week, but now he was doing that in a year. He was down and out. His wife of twenty six years, Irene, had been hounding him now for two years to take a real job somewhere. Their neighbor, Sid Jefferson, had offered to get Barney a job at the hardware store where he could work stocking shelves for minimum wage. The mere thought of punching a timecard made Barney angry. He loved the freedom that real estate had offered him for so many years and there was no way, no how that he was about to report to a boss at this stage in his life.

Irene nagged him constantly. She was stressed because bill collectors called daily looking for credit card and loan payments they just didn't have. She was an innocent bystander to the market, one who watched as The Hasbins' savings slowly and steadily dwindled down to zero. Five years ago, they had it all, including a beautiful beach house on Sewago Lake but that was sold four years ago to pay bills. The last of the money they received from that sale was eaten up during the last winter heating season. What Irene didn't realize was that, like her, Barney was an innocent bystander too. He had no idea that the market would take a downturn that would result in a 75% cut in income. Who could have seen any of it coming? Certainly not Barney. What did she want him to do about it? If he had seen this coming he would have saved better, spent less, and prepared- but he didn't. Barney thought the real estate bubble would never burst and that business would always come his way.

Truthfully, Barney didn't even know why he was still in the real estate business. There was no business out there for him or for anyone. In fact, he went to the office every single day mostly because it allowed him to get away from home and away from the nagging and consistent barrage of questions from Irene.

"Did you find any new customers? Have you talked

to Sid next door about maybe doing some hours at the hardware store? When's your next closing?" It was all too much to take, so Barney came to work each day to hole up in his little cubicle where he perused his emails, collected all kinds of negative information about the economy, stock market, and real estate, from the online media outlets, and commiserated with other agents about the terrible state of the world. He also spent a lot of his day playing online solitaire. Basically, he came to the office to hide.

Today, Barney walked into the building he called work for nineteen years and headed up to the second floor where he could see Summer through the glass door of her office, chatting on the phone with someone. He tapped on her door and she raised a finger indicating she would be just a minute. For a Saturday morning, she looked way too chipper. What did she have to be so happy about?

Summer Straus had been managing the office for just under one year. Rumor had it that she had worked in some type of motivational and coaching industry before coming on board at First Call. Barney didn't like her on day one and his feeling about her continued to descend as the year progressed. Barney especially didn't like that Summer was happy all of the time. She was young and spry with a skinny but toned frame and short blond hair. She'd come to work each day with her bright green eyes and big toothy smile and it just seemed like she was oblivious to the terrible state of the market. If she wasn't oblivious then she was just dumb. Either way, Barney had little respect for her. Besides, Summer Straus was still in grade school when he got his sales license. What did she know about anything?

Jane Eggart, an agent Barney had been sharing a cubicle with for the past two years found some business articles about Summer from three or four years back. Apparently her last company thought she was some kind of coaching genius. She had traveled the world in her past business life where she trained business leaders on how to coach people to greatness. She took the position at First Call Realty after having a baby. The press release that went out internally when Summer joined said that she accepted the position as Manager for First Call because she no longer enjoyed the demands of travelling the world now that she had a family and she welcomed the opportunity that a distressed real estate market could offer to a team of highly skilled and motivated agents.

Summer did her best to motivate and educate the agents at First Call. There were meetings every week and training programs each month. Every Monday Summer would send out an email with motivational tips for the agents. In Barney's opinion, it was all wasted energy on her part. Barney had never attended her meetings or her training programs and he never wasted a second reading her motivational gibberish on Mondays.

Hog wash. That's how Barney saw it anyway. Summer probably knew one of the owners at First Call who gave her the job despite her lack of real estate sales experience. How could some dumb blonde who never sold a house coach a group of real estate agents to be great? The only thing Summer was good at was smiling and being happy all of the time and in this market, that wasn't going to pay the bills for agents who were hit with a recession like none they had ever witnessed. In fact, Summer's cheery demeanor only served to aggravate Barney, and most likely the other agents in the office as well.

Either way, there wasn't much Barney could do about any of it. Summer was his boss whether he liked it or not and when she called him Friday afternoon and asked for a meeting with him Saturday morning he had no choice but to oblige.

"Good Morning, Barney! Great to see you," exclaimed Summer as she opened the door to her office. Despite the fact that it was a Saturday she was in a black suit with her usual pearl necklace, pixie hairdo, and glowing complexion. The sight of her made Barney sick. Maybe it was because he had gained almost forty pounds this past year, taking him to two hundred and fifty pounds, causing him to feel miserable and tired all of the time. Maybe it was because he couldn't pay his bills and could no longer answer his phone at home because it was always a bill collector calling to harass him. Maybe it was because seeing Summer so happy reminded Barney of how miserable he and Irene had become, fighting all of the time about money, work, and their future. The bottom line for Barney was, he didn't like Summer because she represented everything he was not- happy.

"Morning," Barney replied.

"How's life for you? Is there anything I can do to help you in your business or with anything?" asked Summer as she pulled a manila file from her filing cabinet and then relaxed into the black leather chair behind her desk.

"Not unless you can bring the market back to where it was about five , six years ago," replied Barney curtly.

"It's really not that bad out there, Barney. In fact there are many agents making good income right now despite the changes in the market."

"How would you know about the market? You don't sell houses," thought Barney to himself but did not voice. He decided to keep his mouth shut before he ended up saying what was really on his mind.

"I highly respect you Barney. I know that you are good at what you do. You have been in this business for longer than any other sales agent in our firm. You have seen challenging markets before, and you have persevered. This market should have no effect on your business. NONE!" Summer spoke passionately, so much so that she got out of her chair and was pacing the room while Barney sat stoic in his seat.

"No disrespect Ma'am, but you do not know what it is like out there. You have never been in my shoes or any agent's shoes, so please do not speculate. It's a rotten market. There is no business out there at all and when there is no business, there are no sales, which means no money."

"This market reaps opportunity, Barney. Lots of opportunity. I would like to help you get more of it." Summer was still very upbeat and chipper. If she had been affected at all by Barney's forwardness, it did not show.

"Then maybe there is some secret I don't know about, because I just do *not* see it," Barney barked at her.

"There is a secret…that's why I asked you to meet me today." Summer, in her black pumps and business suit, strolled back to sit in her leather chair. She opened the manila file she had placed on her desk and glanced over a single sheet of paper within it as Barney watched her.

"I don't believe in success secrets, *Ma'am*," recanted Barney. He then could not help but add, "Maybe you have been watchin' too many of those infomercials at night." He could feel his blood pressure rising as his hostility at this waste of time grew.

"If you don't believe it, ask Louise Stewart," Summer let out a slight laugh and looked at Barney.

Everyone in First Call Realty knew that Louise Stewart was having a remarkable year in her business. She had been in real estate for four years and this one was, by far, her best. In fact, just this week she had come to work in a new car.

Summer continued, "I shared the secret with Louise in January and now, nine months later, she is busier than she has ever been. In fact, she is in the process of hiring an assistant to help her because she is too busy to do it all herself."

"So, what is the secret?" Now Barney's interest was piqued. After all, Louise did come from out of left field with the stellar year she was having. Maybe there really was a secret. It was doubtful, but maybe.

"I will tell you, Barney, like I told Louise in January, but I need you to do me one favor first." Summer looked at Barney who was looking down at the floor. She was unsure if she was getting through but knew she had to so she continued on. "I can tell you that once you know my Super Sales Success Secret, then you can pretty much count on next year being one of your best ever, and yes, I am well aware that we are not likely going to see a turnaround in the market conditions for several years."

In reality, Barney was in no mood to bargain but just the thought of having some extra cash to pay off the creditors that were calling the house regularly sparked interest for Barney. "What's the favor?" he asked.

"Well, it is not that easy. I can't just tell you the favor." Summer was excited as she knew that Barney's curiosity was a sure sign that he was going to take her offer.

"I don't have time for this," Barney replied. He started to stand and pushed his chair back. He was beginning to dislike his manager even more now that she was trying to get his hopes up with promises of getting his old real estate career back.

"If you don't want the secret, Barney, I will give it to Derek Hoffmann. If you leave this office, the opportunity is lost. Do you want to know the secret or not?"

Derek Hoffmann! Derek was the one agent in the entire company who Barney hated with a passion. Derek was always in the office bragging about how great life was. If for no other reason, Barney wanted the secret so that Derek wouldn't get it.

Summer stood up and handed Barney the manila folder. "Barney, I am going to Tacoma for eight weeks. My sister is having a baby and I'm staying with her to help her through the first couple months. I won't be here to manage and coach the agents."

Barney offered her a blank stare. So, she was going to Tacoma. What did that have to do with him? "Ok," Barney replied.

"While I am gone during that time, anyone can call or email me with problems or concerns. However, I can not be here to mentor, train, and inspire."

Barney rolled his eyes.

Summer continued, " Now, I have a new agent coming on board, a youthful and enthusiastic young man named Eric. He is brand new to this business, recently laid off from a high-tech company. He is eager to do well in real estate and I need you to show him the ropes. With nineteen years of experience, I thought, who better to do the job?"

Barney glanced at the folder and in it was a form with Eric's name, address, and photo. Barney was looking down at a twenty something little punk who woke up one day with a bright idea that he could make millions of dollars selling real estate. This kid was a look alike for that fifteen year old pop star who got famous singing on Youtube. "Not interested," replied Barney.

"Fine, I will go to Derek." Summer picked up her briefcase and was about to leave.

"Then we will end up with two half wits walking around here bragging about how great life is. Fine, I'll train the kid." Barney was agitated and could feel his face was warm. There was nothing he hated more than being backed into a corner. "So, what is the secret?"

"Thank you, Barney. I appreciate your help greatly. Eric will be here on Monday at nine am sharp to start his training. I will be back on the first of December at which time I will share with you my unbelievable Super Sales Success Secret. Your life will change forever, Barney. I guarantee it. Now, I have a plane to catch. Good luck!"

As Summer left her office with a faint stream of perfume trailing behind her, Barney sat there stunned. What had he just agreed to? He was now going to be handcuffed to this moron for eight weeks explaining to him how to be a real estate agent when in actuality the best advice Barney could share was that real estate was the worst possible business to be in. If a nineteen year veteran of the industry could not make money there certainly was no way that a twenty something dreamer was going to. No way, no how. Barney needed to figure out a way to get out of this arrangement, and fast.

CHAPTER 2 –

IRENE

The rest of Barney's weekend was spent doing household chores as he thought about ways to get out of training the new guy. Saturday, Barney mowed his lawn and re-painted the fence outside his modest ranch home he had purchased on Pleasant Street more than two decades ago. By doing so, he thought he would eliminate any need for Irene to nag him about making money. Truth be told he had zero homes under contract and most likely he would not see another paycheck this year. That was just reality. He was a victim of the market and there wasn't much he could do about it.

At dinner Sunday night Barney made the mistake of complaining to Irene about having to train the new guy the next morning. "If you want to get out of having to train him," she reasoned, "Sid will get you a job over at the hardware store. It's nice easy work, Barney, and you'll get *paid*!"

Irene's remark caused Barney to get enraged. Every single conversation they had had over the past five years came back to him getting a job at the hardware store. "I'm sorry I said anything, Irene. I don't want a job at the hardware store. I am a real estate agent."

Irene was heated now too. "Great job that is! You go to work fifty hours a week and bring home NO paycheck. I am the one that has to handle all the collection calls that come in all day. I am the one who has to figure out where we are going to scrape up money for food shopping. I am the one who suffers, Barney, while you go and hide out at your office, for what reason I have no idea."

With this, Barney got up from the table halfway through his meal and left the house. He drove around town for two hours passing by many homes he had sold to clients over the years. He rarely forgot a customer. He could even remember ones who had bought from him nineteen years ago. He was a real estate agent. Real estate was his life. No way, no how, was he going to take a job with Sid working at the hardware store.

By the time Barney arrived back home it was after nine o'clock and Irene was already fast asleep. Barney settled into his recliner in the living room and sifted through the television stations looking for the news. The late night news program he found was one where they were talking about the correlation between increasing crime rates across the country and jobless rates. The entire world was going to hell in a hand basket and Barney drifted off to sleep listening to all the dreadful things happening in the country.

Barney awoke the next morning to the sound of the

television. It was seven o'clock in the morning and he had slept on the recliner all night. Irene had left for work already. Since the beginning of the year, Irene had been working the reception desk at the local hotel. The money she made paid for some of the household bills that Barney could no longer support.

Before rising from the recliner to get ready for work, Barney tuned into the news report on the television. One of the largest auto manufacturers in the country was announcing 5,000 more layoffs by year end. It was more economic doom and gloom for Barney to think about. It just didn't end. What kind of schmuck would want to get into real estate now? Barney just shook his head and got ready for the office.

CHAPTER 3

ERIC

After thinking about things for two days, Barney determined that he was not wasting his precious time showing some dreamer how to sell real estate. Statistically, the odds were against this kid. He could not possibly make it in real estate. Just by listening to the news, everyone knew it was a bad time to buy or sell a house, which meant there just was not any business out there. There was so little business in fact, many good agents, ones in the business for many years, were dropping out of the business like flies. Even when the market was good, it was almost impossible for new agents to jump into real estate and do well. If a seasoned agent like Barney was holding onto his career by the skin of his teeth, what did some newbie think he was going to do to survive?

Barney shuffled into the real estate office at twenty minutes to nine, wearing khaki trousers and an old Champion sweatshirt Irene had bought him. Before he even made it to the coffee pot in the kitchen Derek Hoffmann, a cocky associate whom Barney had tagged in his mind as the office know it all, approached him.

"I listed a gorgeous four bedroom Victorian this weekend if you have any buyers looking," bragged Derek, a tall, lanky, individual who often talked about his college days as a star basketball player.

"No, I don't have anyone. Besides, who wants old Victorians anymore? They all want newer homes." Barney just wanted to get to the coffee.

"Ok, well if you do come across anyone…"

"I won't," barked Barney.

"You know," said Derek. "I have a lot of listings right now. If you want to hold an open house sometime on any of my properties, you can. Might turn into some business for you."

"No."

Barney continued walking to the kitchen. Derek was still talking but Barney had blocked out anything he was saying. Derek was always talking about his new listings. It was like rubbing salt in a wound. Barney did not want to hear it.

As he poured a coffee, Barney thought to himself, if Summer Straus by chance did possess some sort of Super Sales Success Secret, Barney did not want Derek to learn it. Therefore, Barney resigned himself to the fact that he was going to have to comply with Summer's "favor." If only there were a way to comply with Summer's "favor" while at the same time giving the new guy little credence at all.

Young, bouncy, Ginny Talbot, the office administrator,

receptionist, and jack of all trades, came hopping into the kitchen with all the energy of that tiger on the old Winnie The Pooh cartoon.

"Morning, Barney!"

"Morning, Ginny."

"There is a gentleman out front who says he's got an appointment with you," she quipped. "He seems really excited to meet you!"

"Great," mumbled Barney. "Just great."

Barney followed Ginny back to the reception area to meet this appendage he would be stuck with for the next two months.

A man, no older than thirty, stood from the waiting room chair and extended his hand to Barney. Barney accepted the handshake reluctantly as he gave the young man a once over. He wore a double breasted suit, red tie, shiny black shoes, perfectly positioned hair and gold rimmed spectacles. This guy was a bit too much to take.

"Eric Moreland, Sir. Nice to meet you," he said with excitement.

"Are you going to a funeral or something?" asked Barney.

"Excuse me, Sir?"

"Don't call me Sir. My name is Barney. Why are you all dressed up?" Barney was already irritated by the mere presence of Eric.

"Oh, my suit! I have been brushing up on all kinds of fantastic books on how to exceed in sales and one piece of advice I extracted said that you should always dress for the job you want, not the one you have. I want to be the best darn real estate agent this marketplace has ever seen!"

Summer had said that this guy seemed enthusiastic about his new career but she did not say he was so enthusiastic that he was completely annoying. Barney stared at the young man, still not understanding why he was in a full business suit with a brief case and notebook.

Eric elaborated, "I want to be a successful real estate entrepreneur. If I want to run my real estate business as if it were my own Fortune 500 Firm then I figured I better wear a suit to work every single day!" Eric smiled and took in a deep breath. "I know I'm early for my training so if you want to go settle in and return calls or catch up on your voicemails and emails I can wait." Eric's excitement was written all over his face.

"Let's get this over with," Barney grumbled as he walked past Ginny with Eric in tow. Barney could feel eyes on him as he walked past some of the other agents in the office. When he heard one of them snicker he felt like was being played a fool having to deal with this kid. Barney lead Eric down the hall to the conference room and sat him down.

Barney watched bewildered as Eric pulled out and booted up his laptop and prepared his pen and writing pad for notes. Barney secretly laughed inside. *Did he really think I was spending all day with him? What a joke!*

"Kid, do you watch the news?" Barney really wanted to know what would provoke someone to want a real estate career with the state of the current market.

"Not really. No." Eric took out his pen, ready to jot down notes. He felt like he was on the brink of something great as he prepared for his first hours in a new, exciting career, where he would be in charge of his own destiny.

"Well, you should," choked Barney. "The economy is in the dumps. People are scared. Home sales are low. I just thought you should know the truth." Barney figured that if Eric came to his senses and left the business before Summer got back, she would still have to share the Super Sales Success Secret with him. Barney could not control the market which made it impossible for a kid like Eric to survive.

"I studied the home sale statistics for this market area," explained Eric merrily. "I appreciate your being so candid with me though. I want to work with someone that is honest. Summer said we are a perfect match I can already see that she was 100% right! I think this is going to be an amazing eight week mentorship, just like she said!"

"Moron," thought Barney to himself. He then exclaimed sarcastically, "You are a dreamer, kid."

"Thank you," replied Eric.

"Well, let's get this over with. Your first lesson is as follows. You have to tell everyone you know what you do for a living." With that said, Barney left the room and shuffled back to his cubicle for a game of computer solitaire.

Eric wrote down his first lesson on his legal pad. You have to tell everyone you know what you do for a living. When Eric glanced up, Barney was gone so Eric trailed after him excitedly. He found Barney at one of the cubicles in the darkened back room. "Is there anything else for today, Barney?"

"Nope. You are done for the week. That is your lesson. I'll see you next week if you are still in the business."

"Thank you, Sir, I mean, Barney! I will see you the same time, same place, next week! I won't let you down!" Eric could barely wait to put his first week's lesson into play.

"Whatever," Barney mumbled as he placed a four of hearts on top of a five of spades.

Barney was beginning to feel good about his new assignment. In less than five minutes he had managed to dismiss the young real estate dreamer and was able to get back to his daily routine. In fact, Barney had made the lesson up on the spot. In reality, he knew that Eric telling his friends and family that he was now in real estate would do little to nothing for his career. Everyone seemed to know a real estate agent and nobody would care that the world had just licensed another one. The good news was that Barney was fulfilling his side of the bargain. He could not be accused of not doing what he promised to do. This wasn't going to be a bad eight weeks after all.

CHAPTER 4 –

LESSON ONE: TELL EVERYONE YOU KNOW WHAT YOU DO FOR A LIVING

Barney was surprised when, a week later, he came to the office at quarter past nine and noticed Eric sitting at the conference room table as Barney walked back to his desk. Barney had forgotten all about him and the assignment Summer had given him. Subconsciously, Barney assumed Eric had already quit. After all, quitting was in his best interest. The sooner the young man could realize how bad the economy and real estate market were, the sooner he could get out there to start seeking a regular nine to five job.

Barney stepped into the conference room, "You're still here?"

"Good morning, Barney. I picked you up a coffee and donut on the way into work today to say THANK YOU. I worked all week on your first lesson and it is paying off already. Boy, you really do know your stuff!"

Today, Eric was dressed in a grey suit and yellow tie. He appeared to have spreadsheets organized all across the table and Barney was not sure what to make of him, other than the fact that he was irritated by the fact that this guy would delay Barney getting to his computer Solitaire game.

"You should really listen to the news, kid. A report came out last Thursday that said the new construction housing starts were the worst in forty years and foreclosures are at an all time high."

"Thank you, Barney, but I don't see how that news affects me." Eric was standing up and about to explain some of the spreadsheets to Barney.

Barney was angry that Summer had teamed him up with such a naïve imbecile. This kid was so dumb that he could not see the correlation between housing reports and his business. Barney could feel his face turning red yet Eric seemed oblivious. "You're a dreamer, kid," said Barney aloud. He then thought to himself, "and there is no room for dreamers in this awful market."

"Thank you," responded Eric cheerfully.

Barney was not sure how much he could take of this kid. Eric pulled out his spreadsheets and explained that he took last week to comprise a database of every single person he knew in the world. He told Barney how he went through high school yearbooks, college alumni rosters, old employment rosters, and even through the phone book looking for people he had associated with over the last twenty nine years of his life. He told Barney how he tracked down phone numbers and home addresses of folks, many whom he had not contacted in years, and how he called each and every one of them to let them know he had recently begun an exciting career in real estate.

By Thursday afternoon he had reached out to every friend, acquaintance, old soccer buddy, and coach he could remember. Most were just a five or ten minute phone call to catch up on old times while others were meetings for coffee or lunch. Everyone he spoke to was cordial and many were extremely excited about his new venture. All of them promised to keep him in mind if someone they knew were interested in buying or selling a home. Just to make sure they wouldn't lose his number, Eric sent a personal note with business card enclosed to each one thanking them for the opportunity to get reacquainted.

Eric went on to explain that by Friday morning he had contacted every person he knew and he was about to call Barney for help, when he remembered that there was an entire sphere of people with whom he had done business over the years and all those people now needed to know that he was working in real estate too. All day Friday was spent contacting his mechanic, paperboy, gas station attendant, barber, postal carrier, trash collector, dentist, doctor. He contacted local restaurants he patronized and other small businesses he worked with, including the home health care nurses that were taking care of his mom. Anyone with whom he had done business over the past ten years was called on Friday. They too were happy to hear from him and excited about his new career. Again, Eric took the time to follow up every phone call and visit with a personal note which included his business card.

Eric showed Barney how he organized his spreadsheets. There were columns for names, addresses, and phone numbers. While he talked to each person he also collected birthdates for them and their spouses and children. There was then a column indicating the date that he had spoken to the person along with any notes he had about that conversation. Finally, there was a column where Eric marked which people on the list headed to his Facebook Friends. His goal was to befriend anyone on his spreadsheet who was using Facebook since that would make it easy for him to stay on top of what was going on in everyone's lives.

The spreadsheet system was all quite organized but Barney was not that impressed. Barney knew that none of those people would give Eric a real estate lead so it was all just a big waste of time.

"All in all I contacted two hundred thirty seven people last week, including my personal sphere of influence as well as the businesses I patronize. I feel really good about the fact that everyone now knows I am in the real estate business. In fact, an old soccer buddy of mine indicated that his sister may soon be selling her home and he would refer her to me." Eric showed Barney on the spreadsheet where there was a note next to one of the contacts explaining the news about the sister. "I have set a reminder in my calendar to call my soccer friend tomorrow to see if he contacted his sister yet. Can you imagine if I got a deal out of that Barney? It is all thanks to you!" Eric was animated when he talked. His arms moved and he lifted from the seat. He was excited that things were going so well so soon and was grateful for the opportunity to work with some like Barney.

"Well, don't get your hopes up, kid. The market's tough and many sellers don't have equity in their homes. You might think you are getting a lead, but unless you can turn it into a paycheck, it's not a lead." Barney felt as if he were talking to a brick. He could tell nothing was getting through to Eric proving how naïve Eric was about real estate.

"I feel really lucky to have you as my mentor, Barney. You are the best!"

Barney moved to the other side of the conference room as it appeared that Eric was coming at him with his arms wide open.

Barney was too tired to deal with the likes of Eric today. He had a restless sleep the night before. Throughout the previous week, his arguments with Irene worsened to the point that she had made a comment that maybe they were better off divorced. They had fought often in their twenty six years of marriage, but never to the point that divorce had been brought up. Barney was feeling the pressure to make a paycheck. Maybe he would have to bite the bullet and get that part time job after all. Barney committed to scanning the papers to see what was available for part time work, but he was not willing to work at the hardware store with his neighbor, Sid. That being the case, Barney did not have the time to waste dealing with Eric today. Barney needed to get searching for a job. As well, he had to move Eric along in the same direction. The sooner this kid realized that nobody could make a living in a real estate market like this one, the sooner they could both get back to doing their own thing.

"Don't get all hyped up because you contacted two hundred people," Barney grumbled.

"Two hundred and thirty seven, Sir, I mean Barney." Eric was jovial, a pure optimist.

"Fine, don't get excited that you contacted two hundred and thirty seven people, kid, because the likelihood that any of those people will buy or sell a house any time soon is slim to none."

Eric pulled out one of the pages from the spreadsheet he had crafted and walked over to Barney excitedly. "Actually these four names that I highlighted in yellow all said they will be looking to buy and/or sell a home in the next two years!" Eric looked proud.

"Don't be a dreamer, kid. People are not loyal. They will tell you they are going to work with you and then in the end they will stab you in the back and work with someone else." Barney did not have time to be explaining the nuances of this business to someone so adolescent.

"If you look here at my spreadsheet, I have scheduled several follow up calls throughout the year so I can make sure I remain in contact with them until they are ready to buy or sell."

"Spreadsheets will get you nowhere in real life, kid. Stop dreaming. Start realizing that this is a job. One that will not bring you the riches you were hoping for."

"Thank you, Barney. I appreciate that you are so truthful with me." Eric handed Barney the coffee and breakfast he had purchased for him and then prepared his legal pad and laptop for the next lesson.

"Let's get this over with," Barney grumbled, accepting the coffee and Danish.

"The next lesson is this. I told you that telling everyone you know what you do for a living isn't going to bring you all of the business you want. You must now tell the people you don't know what you do for a living."

Eric wrote frantically into his legal pad. "I must now tell the people who don't know who I am what I do for a living." When Eric looked up, Barney was gone already. Eric smiled and thought about what a great guy Barney was for helping him launch his career.

CHAPTER 5

LESSON TWO: TELL PEOPLE THAT DO NOT KNOW YOU WHAT YOU DO FOR A LIVING

Truth be told, Barney didn't even know what exactly his "lesson" meant or how the kid would accomplish it. It made him laugh thinking about Eric passing his business card out to every Tom, Dick and Harry across the state. Like the week before, Barney was in the office every day and Eric never came in leading Barney to hope that he had come to his senses and had finally given up.

Barney had gotten in early today, this time not forgetting that Eric might be in for another lesson. He wondered if Eric had given up, but the kid was so clueless about the industry and the ability for anyone to make money in it, that Barney figured he would be back for week three. It was quarter to eight when Barney got to the office and there was no sign of him yet (which was certainly a *good* sign).

For Barney, things at home were looking up. He and Irene had not had a disagreement all week. Part of this was due to the fact that Irene knew he had scheduled two job interviews for part time evening work. He guessed the fact that he was trying made a big difference to her. Barney went on both interviews, but had yet to hear back from either one. Even if he did hear back from them, he was not necessarily inclined to *take* either position. He had interviewed for the jobs because he had promised it to Irene but that did not mean he had made the decision in his head to accept one. The other reason Irene was less inclined to argue with him was that Barney had gotten a lead for a great listing right in their neighborhood, a result of listening to what Eric had done with his first "lesson".

•••

After his meeting with Eric the previous week, Barney got to thinking. Were there people in his own life that knew him, liked him, and trusted him, but did not know he was still in the real estate business? A nineteen year veteran of real estate, Barney assumed everyone just somehow knew what he did for work. However, Barney did not talk about it often with people so maybe they didn't all know. He decided to start testing the water by casually telling people that he was a real estate agent with First Call Realty.

Last Wednesday, Barney stopped home at lunch to make himself a roast beef sandwich. While eating his lunch and watching a television news report about the increasing unemployment rate, a knock came at the door. It was the postman, Joe Winters, the same postman they had now for about seven years. Barney opened the door and Joe asked him to sign for some registered mail. It was likely a bill collector looking for money. While signing the form, Barney said, "Joe, can I ask you a question," to which he said yes. "We have known one another for about six or seven years now. Did you know that I sell real estate for a living?"

"Now how would I know that," asked Joe. "I mind my own business. Unless people share it on their own, I don't know much about them. "

"Ok, well now you know," said Barney. "If you ever hear of anyone who might need a real estate agent, keep me in mind, would ya?"

"240 Pleasant," replied Joe.

"What's that?" asked Barney.

"The Harrington Family at 240 Pleasant, right down the street, is getting ready to sell their home. I talked to Mrs. Harrington last week. She had some old furniture she put out by the curb with a "FREE" sign and I told my nephew about it. My nephew just moved into a new place. She then offered to give him first dibs on some other items she would soon be giving away as she got ready for her move. I guess her husband's job got relocated."

"Thanks, Joe. I appreciate the heads up."

Just like that, Barney had a lead on a good listing in his own neighborhood. He followed up by visiting Mrs. Harrington to let her know that he would be grateful for the opportunity to talk to her about her upcoming real estate needs. She, in turn, promised that as soon as she was done cleaning out her house over the next couple of weeks, Barney would be given the opportunity to do his sales presentation for her.

●●●

"Barney, Eric is here for you. I told him to meet you in the conference room." It was Ginny, using the intercom button to let Barney know that Eric had not given up. He was here for his week three lesson.

"I brought you a coffee and donut again," said Eric as Barney sauntered into the conference room. " You were right again!" Eric, dressed to the nines once again, in a navy blue suit and tie, was even more ecstatic than last week, if that was even possible.

"Good," responded Barney. "I take it that you finally watched the news and adopted some common sense about this market. You can not make money in real estate sales in this economic climate we are in." Barney fed off the negativity of the media whenever he could, often times without realizing it. He felt solace in knowing that the decimation of his real estate business was not his fault; it was a result of a high unemployment, banks that loaned money to people they shouldn't have, and consumer confidence levels that were in the tank. While eating his breakfast this morning, Barney had the opportunity to read a newspaper article where economists were already predicting that this would be the worst holiday shopping season in twenty years for retailers.

"Oh, not about that. I don't watch that stuff."

Barney could feel his blood pressure rise as he watched more spreadsheets come out of Eric's leather briefcase. He also noticed that now Eric was sporting a gold name tag with his name and First Call Realty emblazoned across it.

"Do not be a dreamer, kid. I'm warning you. What is the goofy pin about? Are you afraid you will lose your jacket? My mother used to sew my name into the collar of my sweaters when I was in grade school for the same reason." Barney didn't mean to make such a mockery of the kid, but it was easy.

"The pin is all part of my plan," replied Eric. "Let me show you what I mean."

For the next thirty minutes Eric went into a long dissertation about everything he had done over the past seven days to follow Barney's latest lesson. He explained all the steps he took to tell people who did not know him that he was proud to be a real estate agent. Eric started by re-contacting all of the people he did know, the ones he had called the week previous, and asked them all for their individual help in referring him to one person they knew who he could talk to for five minutes about what he was doing for work. He was able to connect with fifty percent of his original list and most of them complied by offering Eric a name and number of someone he could call.

Eric did not stop there. He made a simple flyer about himself. It included his photo and his contact information. It explained that if someone were looking for a positive, upbeat, and passionate agent who could demonstrate to anyone why there is no better opportunity than now in the real estate market, they should contact him. Eric explained that he printed one thousand of the flyers and delivered them to local businesses including restaurants, gas stations, convenience stores, and gyms- this time the ones he did not regularly patronize.

On Wednesday, Thursday, and Friday, Eric decided to do what politicians do when they want to tell people that do not know them about who they are and what they do. He started canvassing neighborhoods. In three days, Eric had personally visited over one hundred and twenty homes and spoke with forty two of the owners that were home. He distributed his flyers at each home and when he had the opportunity to talk to someone live he spread the word that this was the best real estate market he had ever seen. Since this was contrary to what the media had been saying for so long, many were willing to listen.

Saturday was spent visiting sellers who were trying to sell their homes on their own, without a real estate agent. He found them by driving around and noticing their homemade signs and by researching the newspapers for their advertisements. For these sellers, Eric printed out some easy home improvement tips from a website online and he dropped them off at each of the properties along with his original flyer. He told the "for sale by owner" sellers that he wanted to share with them the simple home improvement tips because sometimes just little differences in how the house showed could make a big impact on salability. He then relayed to each of the home sellers that if they did eventually decide to contact a real estate agent, he would appreciate it greatly if they would keep him in mind.

Eric was thrilled to tell Barney the most exciting part of the week. "You won't even believe it, Barney. That guy Derek Hoffmann who works on the second floor gave me the opportunity to do an open house at his new Victorian listing. I thought to myself, what better opportunity is there to tell people who don't know me that I am a real estate agent, than at an open house."

Barney was angry that Derek had swindled Eric into doing the open house that Barney had already declined. Barney knew that Derek was not trying to help anyone. He had his own agenda for everything. Derek was probably at the beach Sunday while Eric sat at the open house like a stooge, waiting for buyers to come in.

"You won't even believe this, Barney. A couple came through the open house and they loved it! I started building a great relationship with them and they told me that they are going to work with me to buy a home. I owe Derek a great big thank you!"

This kid just didn't get it. "Great," said Barney. "Just watch your back with people." Barney was referring to Derek Hoffmann. As usually, Eric seemed oblivious to Barney's comment.

Just like the previous week, Eric had documented all of his visits, conversations, and flyer drop offs on his spreadsheets. He had more spreadsheets than a Wall Street bond trader. Barney felt it extremely excessive.

"You are a pure genius," Eric exclaimed with great fervor. "Everything you told me to do is working. I have gotten tremendous feedback and I am already seeing amazing results!"

Barney was more than a bit agitated. This kid just was not giving up which meant this annoying façade would drag on for another week.

"Oh, you asked me about my nametag," Eric reminded Barney. "As I was doing all of this prospecting it occurred to me that I run into strangers every single day, when I am at the food store, Laundromat, or anywhere. I needed a way to tell the world all of the time what I do for a living. I ordered this fantastic nametag and can you believe that the cashier at the donut shop asked me about it this morning? She said that her dad owns a lot of investment properties. By the way, I got his phone number and I will be connecting with him today. The name tag works!"

"It all *seems* easy, kid, but it always seems that way when you are face to face talking to people. They will tell you anything to get you off their case." Barney was not impressed by any stretch. Talking to strangers would not do a thing. The kid was dreaming.

"Oh, I forgot to tell you," said Eric, "when I was prospecting on Marigold Street I stopped at Michelle Walker's house and when I told her I was from First Call Realty, she asked me if I knew you."

"No idea who she is," barked Barney, even though he did vaguely remember the name, and more so the house.

"You sold her that house four years ago," responded Eric. "She said you were wonderful to deal with and she thought that you had retired. I told her that you are still very much involved in real estate and that you were in fact mentoring me."

"Great. I don't remember her," said Barney, lying.

"Well, great news, she is going to be selling her house very soon and she is going to be calling YOU!" Eric was thrilled that he was able to reconnect Barney with a past customer who might soon be listing her home for sale.

Barney was bothered by the fact that Eric was trying to show off. What point was he trying to make? Was he trying to say that Barney was not working hard enough following up with past clients? If Barney only had a vague recollection of this Michelle Walker, there was a decent chance that he had blocked her out of his memory for good reason. Barney's dislike for Eric was growing to hate. He wanted to get rid of him. The kid was a dreamer and a know it all and he did not even listen to the media about what was really going on in the market.

"Barney, did you tell me that your wife works the reception area over at the Doublemore Hotel? Maybe someone here told me. Anyway, when I was canvassing houses I ran into the manager of that hotel and he said his brother is thinking about moving back to this area . Who knows, maybe it will turn into something." In all, Eric got great feedback from four people, including the manager of the hotel and Michelle Walker, who would need a real estate agent in the near future. That was not even counting all the For Sale By Owner homes he had visited, of which he knew many would eventually choose a real estate agent to align with. Eric never thought he would see such positive results so soon.

"You better figure out what is going on out there, kid," barked Barney. Until Eric listened to what the media had to say about the market, he would not learn. It is not like he even had to go far to read or hear all of the awful headlines about unemployment, Wall Street, foreclosures, real estate, and the general economic climate. It was everywhere.

"I am really too busy for this, kid. Go get educated and I will talk to you next week." Barney was angry and he did not even know why. He stormed out of the conference room and right out of the building. He considered calling Summer to let her know he was done wasting his time with this moron.

CHAPTER 6

LESSON THREE: YOU'VE GOT A LOT TO LEARN

After leaving Eric without having given him a lesson last Monday, Barney drove in circles for two hours. He was steaming mad, at what exactly he was unsure. Most likely it was a result of dealing with a young know it all who had no knowledge of how awful the market really was. How could anybody serious about real estate not listen to the news? A tsunami had hit the real estate market and the economy as a whole and everyone out there knew it. The real estate business had come to a grinding halt five years ago for Barney and many other great agents.

Not in the mood to return to his office right away, Barney stopped by the hotel to visit Irene. She was handling a call when he walked through the lobby but after saying goodbye to the caller, Barney, with his voice raised said, "Do these people know I sell real estate for a living?"

Irene was confused. Barney had never visited her at work and now he was asking about whether people at the hotel knew he was selling homes. She was worried that Barney was on the verge of a mental breakdown.

"What are you talking about, honey? I am busy here and I do not think it is a good idea for you to be here."

"What am I talking about?" His voice got louder. "What am I talking about? I am talking about, do you tell people that I sell real estate?"

"Why would I do that, Barney? It is your job to tell people, not mine!"

"Well I will have you know, Irene, that the manager of this hotel has a brother that is moving to the area to buy a home and the sale will be going to someone else at my office and it is all because of you!"

After causing a scene that drew the attention of two people in the lobby, Barney stormed out of the Doublemore Hotel. He drove around the city looking at all the homes he had sold over the years and began questioning his own abilities. It was not Irene's fault that her co-workers didn't know he was in real estate. He knew that deep down. He had never even suggested to her that she should let people know he was a real estate agent. Years ago this would have never happened.

Barney was beginning to see that he is the one who stopped telling people a long time ago that he was in real estate. He could not remember when this occurred, but it did. Maybe it was the year he had sold fifty one houses and was the top salesman for the firm. Maybe it was when the market started to turn sour and deep down he did not want to work so hard anymore. His postal carrier had no idea that he was a real estate agent. His wife's co-workers had no idea that he was a real estate agent. Who else did not know that he could help anyone looking to buy or sell a home? Barney went back to the office to devise a plan.

Throughout the rest of the week Barney put his plan into place. Last Wednesday, at dinner, Irene confided in him that she was worried he was on the verge of a breakdown. When he insisted that all was fine, she asked if he was going to the bars drinking during the day instead of going to work. He assured her that he was not.

Now it was Monday again, and he was at the office early. Eric was due to come in soon, and for the first time since this whole mentorship had begun, Barney actually had a lesson for him, something to make up for the lack of direction he had given Eric the week before.

Eric came in promptly at nine o'clock and set up his laptop in the conference room. Barney met him in there and was not surprised to see that Eric was still dressed in a suit and tie and as anxious as ever to get started.

"Good Morning, Barney! The lesson you gave me last week has been the best yet! I even have some new clients I have to talk to you about."

Barney was confused because he did not give him a lesson last Monday that he could remember.

"The best yet?" Barney questioned the boy.

"Absolutely! You were right, I did have a lot to learn and I went out and got educated just like you said."

"Oh, that. So what? Did you finally see that the market stinks?"

"Oh no, the market is fine." Eric explained all that he had done in seven days to get himself educated about real estate. To begin with, he contacted Louise Stewart. In the past few weeks that Eric had been working at First Call Realty many of the agents had talked about Louise Stewart, a fairly new agent who was having an amazing year in her business, so good in fact that all of the other agents noted the new car she was driving. Eric contacted Louise and offered to buy her lunch for the week if she agreed to let him shadow her so he could see what she was doing to remain so successful.

What struck Eric about Louise was that she was extremely systematized, something that Eric was so far lacking. It was great that he had prepared spreadsheets with contact information for his sphere of influence but so far, he did not have a system to keep in touch with his sphere of influence consistently so that they would not forget to contact him if they were in need of an agent. Eric also lacked a system for reaching people he did not know who might want to utilize his services. A system was one of Louise's key success strategies and so Eric modeled his own system after hers.

Eric showed Barney his new and improved spreadsheet system where he added dates on which he would re-contact his sphere of influence. In essence, he would call every single person on the list every three months. As well, he made a commitment to add five brand new contacts to his list every single day. They had to be people he spoke to personally.

Like Louise, Eric then set up everyone on his database in a news letter campaign. Once a month he would email his database with great information about what was happening in the real estate market and how it affected their ability to buy or sell a home. Of course, in order to do this, Eric did have to take Barney's advice and really study the market dynamics and media coverage of the market. Eric set about collecting articles and news clips about the market. However, it did not stop there. He also had to learn how to use that information in a way that helped potential buyers or sellers make decisions. This was something that Louise did well, and Eric looked forward to putting this information to good use.

There were other systems that Eric set up as well. Everyone on his list would get a card from him on his or her birthday. Every home that was listed for sale by owner in the newspaper or where Eric could see a For Sale sign on display, would receive a visit from Eric. He set up a plan to search for these types of opportunities for thirty minutes every single day. He also prepared a system for dropping off information about himself to all the local businesses on the first of every month, and a system for letting everyone know his perspective on the state of the market through a blog he would update daily.

Like Louise, Eric prepared marketing materials in advance and had them in his car at all times. Louise reminded Eric, "You never know when you will run into your next client."

Eric was already seeing major results, including his first

appointment with someone who wanted to sell her home and buy a new one.

"Sounds like it has been a busy week, kid." Barney was mildly impressed that Eric already had a potential client who wanted to sell her home, but Barney knew from years of experience that an appointment with a potential customer did not mean there would be a paycheck forthcoming.

"It has been fantastic," Eric exclaimed. "And it is all because of you, Barney. I cannot thank you enough! I do have a big favor to ask though."

"What's that?" asked Barney hesitantly.

"I made an appointment to go meet with my new client tomorrow night. She wants to sell her home and buy a bigger one. I told her I would meet her for an initial consultation tomorrow night at seven o'clock. Would you go with me?" Eric was prepared to do it alone but really hoped to have his mentor there to watch him and critique him on his process.

"I will go with you," Barney agreed. "Don't get too excited though. These appointments rarely work out. She is probably just a tire kicker."

"I understand," said Eric.

Barney looked at his watch. He had already been with Eric for over an hour and now had to get ready for his own listing appointment. Mrs. Harrington, referred to him by Joe Winters, the postal carrier, had called Barney to schedule a consultation with him. Barney's entire week was filling out nicely. He was spending time reconnecting with old clients, many he had not talked to since he had sold them their home.

"What is the address of your appointment tomorrow night," asked Barney.

"430 Metropolis Road," replied Eric. "After having spent some time shadowing Louise this week I feel confident in what I have to do. Do you have advice for me, Barney?"

"Stand out," said Barney. "There's a good chance these people will be talking to other real estate agents as well. Make sure you stand out from the rest."

"Got it," exclaimed Eric.

"I'll see you at seven tomorrow at Metropolis Road," said Barney. At that, Barney left to get ready for his own appointments.

CHAPTER 7 –

LESSON FOUR: STAND OUT

Being fall, the leaves on the trees were turning rich colors of red and orange. The air was brisk and at seven o'clock it was already dark out. Barney drove into the driveway at 430 Metropolis at seven o'clock sharp. He pulled in right behind Eric. For the occasion, Barney had dressed in brown trousers and a button down shirt, a significant change from his recent wardrobe of jeans and sweatshirts. He was surprised to find that, for the first time since they had met, Eric was in more casual clothing of khaki pants and a rich green wool sweater.

"What are you doing," asked Barney in a high pitched whisper. "The one time you should be wearing a suit and you are not!"

"She told me not to," said Eric. "She told me to come informal."

Barney noticed that Eric was carrying his trusted briefcase in one arm and a plant in the other. "What is with the plant?"

"It is a clover plant," replied Eric. "It means good luck."

Barney rolled his eyes when Eric turned away. They approached the front door of the well kept ranch. Eric rang the door bell.

Barney did a double take when the woman opened the front door. It was Ginny, the receptionist at First Call Realty, with whom he had worked for many years.

"Ginny? You are selling your home?" Barney was aghast. How did Eric get an appointment with her over any of the other agents who had worked with her for much longer?

As if she read his mind, Ginny said, "Yes, we are expecting our third child next May and we have outgrown our home. Last week, Eric asked me if I knew of anyone who might be looking to buy or sell a home. To be honest I think it was the first time that anyone at the company had ever asked me that. Anyway, I told him YES! Me!"

Barney laughed and shook his head. Ginny brought him and Eric into the living room and offered them coffee. She called her husband, Dave, into the room and made the introductions.

Eric handed his clover plant to Ginny. "This plant represents good luck," explained Eric. "It can't hurt to have luck on our side in the sale of your home and purchase of another." Ginny thanked both Eric and Barney for the sweet gesture.

"I brought something for the kids too," said Eric. Ginny called her two children to the living room while Eric pulled something out of his briefcase. He had brought them both new coloring books and crayons. The kids loved them and Ginny and her husband appreciated that the kids had something to keep them busy while they talked about their home.

For the next hour, Ginny and Dave gave Eric and Barney a tour of the home. Eric took studious notes as they talked and he measured each room with fine detail. Eric asked all the right questions, as if he had been in the business for twenty years. He asked detailed questions about their home and why they had chosen it initially. Ginny and Dave explained that they were only moving because of their expanding family, otherwise they would have lived in the home forever. The two kids never even made a peep. They were fastidiously at work in the other room coloring in their new books.

At the end of the tour, Eric told Ginny and Dave that he would come back at a later time to discuss pricing and marketing strategy, that he would first have to do his homework. Before leaving he offered the homeowners some great materials for them to study on their own. He gave them some graphs which showed in a simple format the state of what the market was like, which illustrated the downturn of the market year over year for four years. Another chart showed the same for average home prices. Eric explained that it was not all bad news because even though the charts looked bad, people were still buying homes out there. Eric printed out some listing sheets of homes in Ginny and Dave's neighborhood that recently sold so they could compare prices on their own, and also gave them some listing sheets for homes that continued to sit on the market due to price. It was a great package that was designed to help educate Ginny and her husband about what was happening with home sales in the area. It would make it easier for them to price properly when Eric scheduled the second appointment.

It was almost nine o'clock when they left the house.

"Good job, kid" A compliment from his mentor was the highest form of flattery Eric could hope for.

"Thanks, Barney. You taught me everything I know."

"I did not tell you to ask Ginny if she were interested in buying a home. I did not instruct you to bring the plant and the coloring books or even the market statistics that you left for them." Barney knew he could take credit for none of it.

"Don't be crazy," Eric retorted. "You were the one who told me to tell everyone what I do for work and you were the one that told me I had to stand out."

Barney shook his head and laughed. "You are a dreamer, kid. Maybe that is not a bad thing"

"I certainly could not stand out with my years of experience," said Eric. "All I could offer was a plant, coloring books, and snapshots of the market. It is so minor compared to what someone like you can offer, Barney. I am just thankful that we work together. I would not want to compete against someone as good as you. That is for sure."

Barney could not wait to get home to ask Irene if she would pick up some coloring books and a clover plant for him. Barney would need them for his next client appointment.

CHAPTER 8 –

LESSON FIVE: BE HONEST

The rest of the week flew by as Barney spent much of his time contacting his old clients. It was greater fun than he could have imagined. Mrs. Amato, an elderly widow to whom he had sold a home seven years earlier invited him in for coffee and fresh banana bread when he stopped by her house on England Street. John and Tracy Bellingham, clients from nine years ago, had since had four children and had easily taken over the three thousand square foot colonial they had purchased. Barney also stopped at the condominium he had sold to a nice young bachelor, Kent McAdams. He had sold Kent the condo he was in because it had just enough room for his pool table. Barney was surprised that Kent had since married and the pool table was replaced by a dining room table.

Throughout the week, Barney had managed to make personal contact with thirteen of his past clients. He reminded them all he was still in the real estate business in case they knew of anyone who needed his assistance and all of them agreed to keep him in mind. It did not just feel good to be out there talking to his past clients, it felt downright great. Barney felt like he had a sense of purpose again in this business.

For every great success story Barney had from the week, there was also a story of failure. Unfortunately, there were five past clients who had moved on without him. This was something he learned when he stopped by to visit only to find another family had moved into the home. Barney was beginning to realize that he had dropped the ball by not staying in touch with his past customers over the years. He had assumed it was a given that they would call him if they needed any real estate help. That was how it had always been in the past. People would just call him when they were ready to buy or sell a home. Barney could not remember when that changed, but it had. All Barney could do now was continue to reconnect with everyone he knew, his past customers, his friends, acquaintances, and even people he did not know.

Eric had scheduled his follow up meeting with Ginny for the following Monday evening. He did it purposely because he wanted to find out his next lesson with Barney before the meeting. Eric found Barney's mentorship to be priceless. Eric, dressed for success, was at the office promptly at nine and Barney was waiting for him in the conference room.

"Thanks for the follow up note card, Eric. You did not have to do that," Barney could hear Ginny talking to Eric as he passed through the reception area.

"Don't be silly, Ginny. I appreciate your confidence in me immensely and I wanted to acknowledge it."

Barney was shaking his head when Eric entered the conference room. "You are good, kid. I have to hand it to you."

"What's that?" asked Eric unassumingly.

"Nice touch with the note card to Ginny," replied Barney.

"Just practicing what you taught me. You are the one who told me to stand out, Barney."

"Summer called me to ask how things are going," said Eric. "I told her better than I could have imagined! I told her that I have been doing everything that you showed me and that this week I have a new buyer, from doing Derek's open house on the Victorian, and that I have a potential new listing on Ginny's house."

"Well, I cannot take the credit, kid," said Barney.

"You deserve all of it," replied Eric. "Oh, Summer wanted me to tell you that she will see you at the end of the month and that she has some Super Sales Success Secret to share with you."

"Ok," said Barney. "By the way, I moved around an appointment so that I can go with you to Ginny's tonight. This is the hard part of the job, where many people give up," said Barney.

"I am ready," replied Eric. "I just wanted to find out what advice you had for me before we go there."

"Be honest," said Barney.

"I am always honest," retorted Eric.

"I am not saying that you are dishonest," responded Barney. "What I mean is that to be a really good sales person you have to be honest with the customer and honest with yourself. You have to be honest with the customer in explaining what you can do for them and honest with yourself in that you should only accept Ginny and her husband as a client if you know that you can help them."

"I don't think I understand," retorted Eric.

"You can't until you have been in the position to," countered Barney. "I will go with you tonight and will do my best to help you through the appointment but suffice it to say that you must keep in the back of your mind that honesty is key, both to your customer and to yourself."

"Ok," said Eric. He could not imagine not being honest with someone but Barney had not let him down yet. Eric knew unequivocally that there was a reason behind the lesson and so he was going to be prepared.

Like the previous week, Barney and Eric showed up at Ginny's house simultaneously at seven o'clock. When they went inside Eric asked if the kids were around and Ginny called them to the living room where Eric presented them each with a printed "Clean Room" award that he had made on his computer. He told the kids that when he toured the home last week he was very impressed that they had put their toys away and that their beds were made. Eric explained to them what an important role they would play should their parents decide to move. Elated with their awards, the kids left the room to go play a game.

For the next thirty minutes Eric went over the market analysis report he had prepared with Ginny and Dave while Barney sat back and listened. Eric was confident that the home would sell for between $300,000 and $310,000 and he had plenty of proof to support it including two sales right on the same street. As Eric discussed his pricing strategy, Barney could feel the tension in the air thicken. Ginny and Dave glanced at one another nervously and Ginny sank back into the couch and crossed her arms. Her laid back demeanor shifted and it was apparent that she did not like the information that Eric was sharing.

"That won't work for us," said Ginny coldly. "We need $375,000 and we know our home is worth it."

Eric looked at his report as if he were ready to go back in and justify his numbers. Barney was prepared to step in but first wanted to give Eric the opportunity to handle things on his own.

Ginny continued, "We have over an acre of land, four bathrooms, a pool, a garage, granite countertops in the kitchen, a wonderful location, in an area that people would die for!" Ginny's voice was rising in tandem with her irritability at the situation.

As Ginny continued to list all the wonderful attributes to the home, Eric began to second guess his estimate. He had examined all the comparable homes at length. He knew every house that was on the market and every house that sold in the area. He also knew all the ones that did not sell despite their long history on the market. Eric did not know what to do. He had never expected that Ginny would get upset at him. Should he offer to go back and do the numbers again? Should he offer to list her home for $375,000 because that is how she saw the value? Maybe he was not cut out for this job after all. For the first time, Eric really began to doubt his abilities.

When Ginny finished explaining her point, Dave then

expressed his own thoughts. He too felt the house was worth more and reiterated some of the points about the home that Ginny had relayed.

Eric looked over at Barney who was witnessing the scene. Eric felt like he was letting him down immensely and he quickly recapped in his head each of the lessons. It then occurred to him what Barney had told him earlier. Be honest. Be honest with your client and with yourself. He now understood what his great mentor was trying to teach him. This gave Eric the confidence he needed to take control of the situation.

Calmly, Eric spoke. "I have to be honest with you, Ginny and Dave. I did consider all of the wonderful attributes you just recited when I was pricing out your home. Every feature you just shared with me is similar to those in the home located at 501 Metropolis Road, right down the street. That home sold three months ago for $300,000. The houses are very similar. I feel you have a more favorable lot because your house sits off the street and is a bit more private so it is possible we will get slightly more than $300,000. However, we are coming into a slower time of year so it is also possible that you will get lower than they did." Eric handed them the feature sheet for the house at 501 Metropolis so that they could compare the characteristics of the two homes. Ginny and Dave read the sheet closely.

"The house right down the street is on the market for $360,000," said Ginny, "and it is not even half as nice as our home."

"This home," asked Eric as he handed them a feature sheet for a split level home right down the street from Ginny and Dave's.

"Yes, that is the one," agreed Ginny." That one is so much smaller and needs a lot of work."

"That house has been on the market for three years and they continue to drop the price," explained Eric. "It will not sell for anywhere close to what they are asking for it. Unfortunately for them they do not have a real estate agent who is willing to be honest with them."

Ginny and Dave remained quiet as they examined the feature sheets that Eric had offered them.

"Wow," said Ginny. "We are really shocked by this."

Eric opened up his briefcase and pulled out what appeared to be an x-ray of a bone. Barney, who was impressed with how Eric had handled himself so far was now getting nervous. What was Eric up to with the x-ray of a bone?

"Ginny, Dave, do you know what this is?"

"It looks like an x-ray," said Dave inquisitively.

Eric leaned forward toward Ginny and Dave and pushed his wire rim glasses up higher on the bridge of his nose as he prepared to explain to them the importance of the x-ray. "Yes, I play soccer in an under thirty league on the weekends and I fractured my foot playing two years ago. When I went to the doctor that Saturday and they took the x-ray the doctor showed me the fracture." Eric pointed at a grey line across the bone. "I kept telling the doctor he had to be wrong because I did not want to be on the sideline for the entire season. The doctor pointed to the line on the x-ray clearly illustrating a fracture and he said, "This is the fracture, and there is nothing I can do to change it."

Barney was not the only one in the room who could not see the point Eric was trying to make.

Eric held the market analysis report up next to the x-ray. "This market analysis report on your home is exactly like the x-ray of my broken foot. It is the result of a market that you and I have no control over. For us, the market is that grey fracture line. Our market has taken an extensive hit over these past five years and the value of your home has little correlation to what you paid for it, the great characteristics it has, or to the fine upgrades you have made over the years. Instead, your home is the product of a difficult real estate market and what a consumer will pay for it as compared to all of the other homes that are available for sale. I wish I could tell you that your home is worth $375,000. I wish I could. I would not be honest with you if I did. I also would not be honest with myself if I were to sign a contract saying I could help sell your home for that price. This market analysis is our x-ray of the market and today's market will only support a price of $300,000 to $310,000."

Barney was more than impressed. Apparently so were Ginny and Dave. They appeared to relax and they began to continue the dialogue about getting their home ready to put on the market.

"How long will it take us to sell at your price," asked Ginny. Her arms were relaxed along her side and it appeared that she was accepting the reality of what Eric had shared with her.

"I cannot promise anything but I think if you price it in the $300,000 range you can expect an offer in the next thirty days. Of course, the market is always changing. Therefore, it could take longer."

"Ok," said Ginny.

"I almost forgot to share the good news with you," said Eric.

"It is hard to believe there is any," sighed Ginny.

"There is some really good news," said Eric.

Barney was not sure where Eric was going with this but was listening intently.

Eric continued, "I did some research on the type of home you are looking to buy. You told me that you are interested in a four bedroom colonial in the west side of town. You told me you need a kitchen with plenty of cabinets and would like a big yard."

"And a garage," Dave reminded everyone.

"And a garage," validated Eric. "Well, you should look in the $400,000 to $420,000 price range if you want a house that has all that."

"We qualify for that," replied Ginny.

"But the good news," said Eric, "Is that if you had shopped for this same type of home three years ago, you would have had to be in the $520,000 to $550,000 price range to find a home with those characteristics. There is a silver lining to the market we are experiencing today," said Eric in an excited tone. "You are saving a lot of money as a buyer."

"That is fantastic news," said Ginny and her husband agreed.

The rest of the meeting went better than expected. Eric listed the home for $305,000. Ginny and Dave were in great spirits as Eric explained how the entire process would take place.

"I will keep you and Dave informed of all scheduled

showings. I will also follow up with each real estate agent who shows your home to gather any feedback they and their customers have. I will make sure you are comfortable that you are making good decisions every step of the way. It's important that we work as a team." From there, Eric explained all of the work he would do to get the property market ready: install a lockbox, prepare marketing sheets, schedule open houses, draft advertising pieces, and more.

It was after nine o'clock when Barney and Eric left. Barney congratulated Eric on a job well done and promised to meet with Eric throughout the week to help him with his new listing. It was not Barney's client and it was not his new listing, but he felt so good that it may as well have been.

CHAPTER 9

LESSON SIX: BE ACCOUNTABLE

After watching Eric in action at Ginny's house, Barney went home and went directly to his basement. Irene came down at eleven o'clock at night and was incredulous at the sight before her. The bankers boxes with years of tax records, medical records, holiday ornaments, and everything else they stored were all opened and spread in disarray across the floor.

"What on earth! Have you lost your mind, Barney?" It was rare for Irene to raise her voice, but at this she just couldn't help it.

"I am looking for something, honey. I feel like things are changing for me." Barney was coming off of his high from listing Ginny's home and knew he could not go to sleep.

"You have lost your mind!"

"Honey, I will clean it up. Please don't worry. I promise

I will clean it." Barney was oblivious as to the level of anger Irene was projecting.

"You are darn right you are going to clean it!"

"Do you remember when I fell off the ladder painting the front of the house nine years ago," asked Barney to Irene.

"Yes, Barney. It was one of the rare times you helped with housework. How could I forget?"

"Don't be like that, Irene. I feel like things are really changing for us. I need the x-ray from my wrist. I know it is in one of these boxes."

"You need what?"

"My wrist x-ray."

"You really have lost it Barney. Good night." Irene stormed up the stairs and for the rest of the week she remained distant. By Saturday, Irene had recovered and had approached Barney at breakfast to let him know that she might have a customer for him. At Barney's insistence she started telling some of her co-workers that he was in real estate. It turns out that Irene's shift manager, Clara, had been renting an apartment for some time. Recently engaged, Clara was wondering about her buying options. Barney was thrilled when Irene shared the news with him.

Barney did find the x-ray from his wrist and he did take it on his second appointment with Mrs. Harrington, the customer that was referred to him by his postal carrier. Mrs. Harrington too was disappointed that the value of her house had dropped. Like Eric, Barney explained that the market analysis he had prepared was a result of his taking a snapshot of today's market. Like a doctor cannot control what the x-ray shows, nor could Barney, as a real estate agent, control the prices resulting from a challenging real estate market. Mrs. Harrington appreciated the analogy and she listed her home at 204 Pleasant with Barney at a good price which would result in a fast sale. Barney was starting to look at the challenging economic climate as a great opportunity for good agents to shine.

Barney and Eric met the following Monday. Barney called Eric throughout the week to offer him assistance with Ginny's listing but it appeared that Eric had everything under control. When Eric arrived in the conference room, dressed in his suit and tie, Barney was not yet sure what the lesson would be. The truth was, Barney felt he was learning more from Eric than Barney was able to teach Eric.

"So, how are you doing on Ginny's listing," wondered Barney.

"Not so great," said Eric. "There has been zero interest in the property so far. Nobody is calling to look at it and I just don't know what to tell her. I do not even like coming into the office because I know she will ask for a status report each time."

"Have you done all the things you told her you were going to do? Did you prepare listing flyers, schedule open houses, install a lockbox, put the sign up?"

"To tell you the truth, Barney, I have not done anything yet only because there has not been any interest in the home. Once I get a call on it, I can get all of that done within a few hours."

"It does not work like that, kid. If you want to be the best, you must follow through on every detail of what you said you would do, no matter what. You are accountable for your promises. If you do not follow through, you will lose trust with your client."

"I didn't think of it like that," exclaimed Eric. "I just figured there was no rush yet."

"You should always feel a sense of urgency when it comes to your accountability. Just do what you said you were going to do and you won't have to feel uncomfortable coming into the office to face Ginny." At that, Barney excused himself and explained to Eric that he was heading out to meet Irene at the hotel so that she could introduce him to Clara, the shift manager interested in buying a home. Barney was going to offer to let Eric come along for the ride but it sounded like he would have his work cut out for him catching up on all the things he had promised to do for Ginny.

Barney felt like there was a shift in the local real estate market. In the past week, he had listed the Harrington's home at 204 Pleasant. As well, he showed three homes to a first time buyer, a referral from one of his prior clients whom he had recently contacted. The Barney Hasbin who had spent the previous four years of his career complaining, spreading negativity, and stuck in a rut of self pity and loathing, was now spending most of his days visiting his vast array of old friends, acquaintances, and past clients. His office computer, which was previously used for nothing more than computer solitaire was now an important tool used for updating and tracking his database. Barney was realizing the cause behind his complacent life and ruined real estate career. Himself.

When Barney came back from The Doublemore Hotel

he was on cloud nine. He was in such a good mood that he stopped at the bakery and bought pastries for the entire office. When Ginny inquired as to why he was so thrilled, Barney explained that he had just signed a buyer contract with a new client, Clara, who was even more motivated to buy a home than Irene originally thought. "Barney Hasbin is back in business," exclaimed Barney.

"I am pretty happy too," said Ginny. "You would not believe all of the great things Eric is doing to get my house sold. He made beautiful marketing sheets. He printed hundreds of them and left them at all of the local businesses in town. He even canvassed my neighborhood to see if anyone on my street had a friend or relative that might be interested in buying my house."

"Nice touch," said Barney. "You have got yourself an A+ real estate agent."

"I know," said Ginny. "He is doing so much for us and my husband and I are really thankful."

As Barney was walking back to his cubicle to make a list of homes for his new buyer to look at, Eric walked in. His suit looked worn and his tie was lose.

"You walk through a wind storm or something?" asked Barney.

"No, I just had so much to do to come through on my word for Ginny. I put a For Sale sign up and prepared the listing flyers. I have spent the entire afternoon canvassing the town telling people about her listing."

"That is incredible."

"Not that incredible," retorted Eric. "Nobody is interested in her house."

"As long as you can go to bed at night knowing that you have done absolutely everything you promised to do for your client, then there is nothing more that you can do. We are in a challenging market and these things take time and patience."

"I guess," said Eric discouraged.

"Something good will come out of all of your hard work. Trust me."

"I know. When I was canvassing neighborhoods telling them about Ginny's home I met two people that want to sell their homes. They were impressed with the effort I was making for Ginny and both have asked me to do presentations for them on their homes."

"Two more clients!"

"I know, it is great," said Eric, "But I really want to get Ginny's house sold."

"Be patient and keep doing what you are doing," replied Barney. "It will all work out in the end."

CHAPTER 10 –

LESSON SEVEN: NO GIVING UP

After the busiest week Barney had seen in years, he met with Eric first thing Monday morning. Eric looked tired and his usual energetic persona had dissipated. Barney noted the irony to himself. It was less than two months ago that he and Eric had met for the first time in this very conference room when Eric was the picture of positive energy and happiness and when Barney was the negative mope that was all but ready to give up on his career.

"You were right, Barney. This is harder than I thought. I wanted you to know that I am weighing my options right now."

"Weighing your options? What does that mean?"

Eric replied longingly, "I am not cut out for this. I am interviewing for jobs, something that does not involve disappointing people."

"That is ridiculous," cried Barney. "How many potential client appointments have you had in the past six weeks since you started?"

"Six," replied Eric.

"How many buyers are you now working with?"

"Four."

"How many people have you talked with and added to your database?"

"A few hundred."

"Eric, you are incredibly good at this job. You are in the business of helping people achieve one of their biggest dreams, buying a home. For most people it is the single largest investment they will make in their entire lifetime. You cannot expect that to be an easy job."

"I guess," said Eric, "But, I really feel like I was just dreaming big as usual when I set out to start this career."

"You are a dreamer, kid. That is not a bad thing. In fact, I have been thinking a lot lately about my past nineteen years in this business. The biggest thing I had when I started was my dream. I wanted to be great and it is all I ever thought about. When I started in this business there was no stopping me. I focused on achieving me dreams and that is exactly what I did. I was a dreamer, kid. Just like you."

Barney continued, " Let's face it, you are doing better than most real estate agents in the business right now. Why? For one, you work harder than everyone else. You get out there and spread the word about who you are and what you do. The other reason you are unbelievable is that your positive mental attitude about everything causes you to keep going when everyone else is giving up. You are focused on your dreams and if you stay that way, you will achieve them all."

"There *is* great opportunity out there," said Eric. "I know that there is opportunity."

"That's the right attitude," said Barney.

"I do have some big dreams I want to achieve," said Eric. More to himself than to Barney.

"This week your lesson is Don't Give Up. Continue to persevere by finding opportunity where others cannot see it. *You* taught me that, Eric. I had all but given up on my career until you came along. By watching you I was able to see that my worst enemy was not the real estate market. My biggest enemy was me. My negativity had ruined my career. I learned from you, Eric, that I had to stop listening to naysayers, the biggest one being the news. I do not want to give up on my career, Eric. I do not want to give up on it because you taught me that there is incredible opportunity to succeed in this market regardless of what the economy is like."

Eric just stared at Barney as he processed everything he was saying.

"I am a dreamer again, kid. It is because of you." Barney was realizing that maybe there was a reason Summer Straus had such raving reviews about her coaching abilities. She knew exactly what she was doing when she teamed up Barney with his student.

"But, I feel like I am letting Ginny down because nobody is looking at her home. I have done everything I possibly can to draw attention from the public but nothing is working. If this is what it is like every time I cannot do it."

"That is going to happen sometimes, kid. The market is temperamental and we cannot control it. What we can control is our attitude. Keep doing all the great things you have been doing, kid. It will pay off. Look at me. I have become a dreamer again and my business is really starting to take off!"

"I am just in this rut," said Eric.

"We all get in ruts. Just make sure yours does not last five years like mine." Barney continued, "You are a master at turning negative information into positive."

"I don't think I know what you mean, sir."

"When we were at that second meeting with Ginny and her husband you took some pretty negative news articles about the economy and real estate market and you used them as a tool for your business. It was like you were a soldier in combat and when you needed the right weapon you just went right into your arsenal and grabbed the appropriate one."

"I guess," said Eric.

"There are lots of sales people out there right now who are listening to the negativity out there and letting it get them down. Look at me. It almost destroyed me and my business. You used the negativity as a tool to show your client how to sell her home."

"I didn't look at it like that," replied Eric. "Well, the good news is that if Ginny's house is not selling even though it is priced competitively, that means that it is likely that the home she will move up to is also sitting on the market. She might have to take a hit of ten percent on her price but most likely she will save ten percent on the home she is moving up to. In the end it works out to be better for Ginny."

"That's the right attitude!"

"You are right Barney. I am going to stay positive and simply not give up! By the way, you look like a million bucks," said Eric as he nodded toward Barney's attire.

Barney had practically forgotten that he had worn a suit today. He had not worn it since his daughter's wedding three years earlier and it was a little tight around the waist, but it felt good to put it on. He felt like he had purpose. In fact he did have purpose, he had some dreams he wanted to achieve. The first of which was getting his real estate career back, and he was well on his way.

Late last week, Barney stopped by Doug and Joanie Doucette's home. They had bought their home on Wilshire Circle in Dundee Falls through Barney more than ten years ago. Barney stopped by to say hello and to apologize for not keeping in touch. It turned out that Joanie's arthritis was getting the best of her and she was disappointed that she would not be able to decorate her yard with lights for the holidays. Barney so enjoyed seeing his old clients that he stayed and talked with them for over an hour. When he went home and talked to Irene about seeing Doug and Joanie, Irene suggested that the two of them could go to the Doucettes' while they were at church on Sunday and put up their holiday lights and that is just what they did.

Barney enjoyed spending Sunday with Irene decorating the Doucettes' with holiday lights of all colors. Barney felt better than he had in years. For his career, he felt promise and hope. For his personal life, he felt happy and content.

Irene felt it too. Irene had purchased the Doucette's a holiday wreath for their front door. As she hung it, she told Barney that she was proud of him and everything he was doing to change their situation. Barney couldn't remember anyone ever telling him that they were proud of him. That it came from his wife of twenty six years was touching. Irene was happy to see him wearing suits again, going on client appointments, and making a concerted effort to help home buyers and sellers achieve their dreams. All he seemed to talk about lately were the people he was reconnecting with and the great success he was having in doing so. In fact, as of recently, Irene noticed that Barney was not even watching news programs at night and was instead reading motivational books. He had even started to go on a short walk every morning before work. Life was good. In fact, Barney and Irene agreed life was better than it had been in years.

When the Doucette's returned home and witnessed what Barney and Irene had done for them they were moved. Joanie started crying and she hugged both Irene and Barney over and over. Joanie insisted that Barney and Irene join them at their parish that evening for a potluck dinner. The Barney of old would have declined before even thinking about it. The Barney of new, considered it, looked at Irene who he knew would want to attend, and said "Sure! Why not? We have never been to a potluck dinner."

The dinner was fantastic. There were about thirty people from town who attended and Joanie spread the word about how her friends, Barney and Irene, had taken it upon themselves to decorate her yard with the most beautiful holiday lights, since her arthritis had hindered her ability to do it. This ended up being the talk of the evening and the entire group of them decided to form a parish committee to help people around town who were handicapped in some way. They would provide yard work, home repairs, and even transportation to shopping, doctor appointments, or just anywhere for those who could not drive. Barney and Irene were amazed at how one good deed could turn out into a catalyst that would help hundreds of local citizens.

The parishioners wasted little time. They formed their committee and asked Barney to be the head of it. They named it the Helping Hands Committee. Their first meeting was that night at six o'clock. Barney wanted to look good for his new role- hence the suit. Besides, he had also scheduled an early afternoon client appointment, a referral from a previous customer whom Barney had visited two weeks earlier. Barney could not promise anyone that he would wear a suit every day, but it felt so good wearing one, that he was confident it would become an important part of his wardrobe.

Barney could not believe how much his world had changed in seven short weeks. He owed great thanks to Eric, and to Summer for matching them up.

CHAPTER 11

THE FINAL LESSON: THE SUPER SALES SUCCESS SECRET

When Barney walked through the front door of his office the following Monday morning he could feel a positive buzz in the air. Maybe it was because he had sold a house the previous weekend and would have a much needed payday to look forward to. Maybe it was because Ginny had announced to him, "I got an offer," in an excited bellow as he walked past her front office station. Maybe it was because the first meeting of the Helping Hands Committee at the new parish he would now be attending regularly went unbelievably well. Whatever it was, there was a positive energy- so much so that it was almost palpable.

As Barney made his way back to his cubicle he was stopped in his tracks by a bright, cheery, well tanned

Summer Straus who popped out of her office and said, "Hi stranger, I'm back!"

Summer looked at Barney puzzled and said, "Wow! You really are a stranger. Nice suit!"

Barney had completely forgotten that Summer was due back already. It seemed like Eric had just started with the First Call Realty and Barney felt a sense of disappointment at the possibility of not getting to work with him any longer.

"How is business?" asked Summer.

"Doing well," replied Barney. "In fact I sold a home this weekend. I have three houses I am currently marketing and several very good prospects for business in the New Year."

"Right on!" screamed Summer slapping Barney on the back. "I am so proud of you, Barney!"

There it was again. In all these years nobody had said they were proud of him and now in just a week's time he had heard it from both Irene and now Summer. Barney did not feel like he had done anything special but he could feel the positive changes taking affect in his life. He felt emotional when Summer said she was proud.

"The market is really good," said Barney.

"Did I just hear Barney Hasbin say the market is good? Did I really hear that correctly?" Summer poked him in the arm in jest.

"It is good," said Barney with a shrug.

"That is not what I heard on the news on the way over," tested Summer smiling.

"What do they know? The market's between your ears. If you think it is good, it is good. If you think it is bad, it is bad."

"Right you are Barney! Where is Eric? I owe you guys something."

Barney looked at Summer quizzically. What did she owe him?

"The Super Sales Success Secret," announced Summer. "You guys earned it!"

"Oh, that. I almost forgot about it," laughed Barney.

"Well, it is an important secret that will change your life."

"Don't worry about Eric, he will be along any minute. He is predictable like that. Any pictures of the baby?"

"Who?"

"The baby! Didn't your sister have a baby? It was the reason you left us for a while. I would love to see some pictures."

There was no need to ask twice as Summer had an entire album full of pictures of her new niece, Baby Elizabeth. She shared her photos with Barney and other agents in the office stopped by to look at them too. Yes, that positive buzz was electric, absolutely electric.

After ten minutes Eric came striding down the hallway with a lift to each step. It was the happy, positive Eric that Barney admired. "Did you hear we got an offer on Ginny's place?" announced Eric cheerily.

"I did. Congratulations! I told you that you were making all the right moves."

"Thanks, Barney. The offer is a good one. They are probably going to accept it. Now I have to get them out this week to find a home to buy!"

"That is fantastic, Eric." Knowing how good the words felt, Barney said, "I am proud of you!"

Summer gave Eric a hug and congratulated him on his first transaction. She then invited both Barney and Eric into her office for a private meeting, door closed.

"So, you guys are busy. That is fantastic! I was out in Tacoma visiting my sister and the real estate market there is pretty tough. You two have outsmarted the market here!"

Barney and Eric looked at one another and smiled.

"That is exactly what I thought would happen," said Summer.

Barney and Eric looked at each other again, this time with confused expressions.

"It was?" asked Barney.

"Absolutely. I know the Super Sales Success Secret in business and in life and I put it to work on you two. I have seen it work hundreds of times and I am happy to see that it worked on you too."

A big grin occupied most of Summer's face. She was obviously proud of her accomplishment.

"Don't you guys see what you have done for one another?"

"No, I don't see anything," replied Eric, confused.

"You don't see it?" Summer thought it was beyond obvious. "Eric, did you learn anything at all from Barney?"

"Of course, he taught me everything I know. He taught me how to tell the people I know, and those that I do not, about what I do. He taught me how to go out and educate myself about the market and about the business and he showed me how important it is to stand out and to be accountable for what I do. He showed me the importance of never giving up. I owe all of my success to Barney. I really do!"

Barney was flattered. He could not imagine that he would have such great impact on someone else's career.

"Barney, did you get anything out of these past couple of months?" Summer was obviously trying to make a point. What that was, Barney was unsure.

"Sure I did. I learned that all that stuff that he supposedly learned from me really works. Look at him, he is doing an unbelievable job. I also learned that I am not a product of the market. In fact, I am choosing NOT to participate in the recession we are in. Finally, I learned that being positive and upbeat is a game changer in my career. It feels good to let go of the negativity."

Summer sat behind her desk staring at the two men.

Barney continued, "Oh, I learned that it does not hurt to dress sharp too. I mean, I have got to be prepared to do business at any moment, so I might as well dress like I am ready for it!" Barney winked at Eric and Eric nodded in return.

"Ok, so I guess I am going to have to spell it out for you guys. Don't you see that by helping others, you automatically elevate your own game?"

Both Barney and Eric were now beginning to see her point.

Summer continued, "You both know that I read a lot of books. One of my favorite writers and speakers is Zig Ziglar.

He has a quote that says if you help enough people get what they want, you will in turn get what you want."

Barney and Eric looked at one another. For the past eight weeks they had, in some way, helped each other get what they wanted, a great career in real estate. Neither of them had even realized what they were doing.

"Barney, before Eric came along you were happy just living the status quo. You were dwelling in misery and letting the market get the best of you. I had to nudge you a little to help Eric, but as you helped him, you started seeing positive results in your own life."

Barney was amazed, or more like awestruck. She was absolutely right. He had transformed his mind, his business, and his life, all while in the process of helping Eric.

"Eric," said Summer, "you did the same for Barney. By demonstrating to Barney that someone brand new could come into this business and have success immediately, as a result of hard work and positive attitude, you helped Barney see how to get back on track in his life."

Eric was taken back. He had no idea that he had impacted Barney in that way.

"Without each other, neither of you would have been successful. The Super Sales Success Secret is to help others get what they want, and you will get what you want!"

"Wow," said Barney. "That is amazing." Barney was now thinking about how this secret was taking affect in other areas of his life. By helping Joanie Doucette with her holiday lights, he was able to make great friends and acquaintances at the parish. This would allow him to meet more people through the new Helping Hands Committee. The more people he could help, the more business he would be able to do in real estate. It was all about helping people while forming great relationships within the community.

"I am amazed," said Barney to Summer. "I was so negative on this business, and you took a big risk on me. I could have easily discouraged Eric to quit on day one. In fact, that is what I *wanted* on day one!"

"I knew my plan would work fine on you Barney. I knew it for sure."

"You did?"

Summer got up from behind her desk and got a manila file out of her cabinet. This time it was Barney's personnel file. From it, she took out what looked like a really old advertisement that Barney had run in the local newspaper. "Do you recognize this?"

"Yes, it is an old advertisement I ran in the newspaper many years ago to attract business." Barney was confused as to what point she was trying to make.

"What does the tag line at the bottom say," asked Summer.

Barney read it aloud, "Call Barney Hasbin for your real estate needs. *Achieving my dreams, by helping you achieve yours.*" Barney now vaguely remembered having great success with the advertisement.

"When I saw that advertisement, Barney, I knew that you understood the principle of helping others achieve what they want as a means for achieving what you want. In fact, you understood it long before most of us did. I just needed to nudge you in the right direction!"

"You are both pretty amazing. Barney, you really were a dreamer," said Eric.

"Yes, I was," replied Barney. "I am a dreamer."

"By the way," said Summer, "I teamed up Louise Stewart and Derek Hoffmann in January and they both understand and practice the Super Sales Success Secret.

"They do," said Barney. Something then dawned on him that made him feel terrible, and really embarrassed. "So, when Derek was offering to let me do his open house, he was really trying to help me?"

"Of course," replied Summer. "Why else would he offer to let you do an open house on that gorgeous new listing?"

Barney owed a big apology to Derek, and probably others too.

Eric then opened a bag he had carried in with him and took out a small box that he handed to Barney. "I got you a little something, just to say thanks for everything you have done for me."

"Oh, kid, you shouldn't have done that. I haven't really done anything."

"Just open it," said Eric. "It is just a small token to say thank you."

Barney opened the box and, even though it was a small gift, it meant the world to Barney. He could feel tears welling up in his eyes. The gift, a gold emblazoned name tag which read *"Barney Hasbin - First Call Realty – How Can I Help You?"*

The Eight Lessons To Sales Success A Great Salesman Did Not Know He Knew

Lesson One: Tell Everyone You Know
What You Do For a Living

Lesson Two: Tell People That Do Not Know
You What You Do For A Living

Lesson Three: You've Got A Lot To Learn

Lesson Four: Stand Out

Lesson Five: Be Honest

Lesson Six: Be Accountable

Lesson Seven: No Giving Up

The Final Lesson: Help Others Get What They
Want, You Will Get What You Want

My Short List of Recommended Personal Achievement Sites:

www.MyRandomActsofCardness.com

www.P3Coaching.com

www.LittleThingsMatter.com

www.LittlePinkBook.com

www.Happiness-Project.com

Contact Stacey:

Stacey Alcorn

P3 Coaching

2100 Lakeview Ave

Dracut, MA 01826

Stacey@PeakPandP.com

Peak
Performance
Profitability

P3 Coaching is dedicated to empowering professionals to be their best

Visit Our Website and Explore – www.P3Coaching.com

Consulting: P3 Coaching offers a wide arrange of specifically tailored products for virtually every profession including real estate agents, mortgage originators, sales professionals of all kinds and self employed entrepreneurs.

Speaking: Do you have a sales force that needs some pumping up? How about managers or team leaders that need to realize that greatness is within reach? The P3 Coaching team offers several half-day or full-day motivational programs tailored to various industries. The P3 Coaching programs are perfect for companies that need to "next level" their salespeople, consultants, and managers to become leaders within their own individual positions within the organization.

Products: Take a look at the amazing arsenal of personal empowerment products available through P3 Coaching including several books on leadership, management, recruiting, salesmanship, time management, and work/life balance. As well, visit the full line of coaching and training programs geared toward specific industries.

www.P3Coaching.com

Made in the USA
Columbia, SC
21 January 2020